TULSA
A Celebration

TULSA
A Celebration

TULSA
A Celebration

I would like to thank the following people for their continued support of Novel Idea Books and their help with putting this book together: Patti Ledford, Nancy Godsey, Thom Golden, Dee Hausam, Tom Dyer, Keely Davis, Rita Fowlkes, Paula Wells, Karla Taylor, Stephanie Howerton, Debbi Cadieux, Sue Mitchell, Susan Coman, and Jane Podpechan.

HOWARD DOAK

The majority of the photos for this book were taken by Nancy Godsey with the exception of the following, which were taken by Rick Stiller: (In order of appearance): Cover Photo, Pumpkins, Buffalo, Fall Leaves, Holy Family, Skelly Mansion, Atlas Building, Williams Tower, Fountain, Philbrook, Downtown at Night, Holland Lakes, Winter in Tulsa, Philharmonic, Will Rogers, Flowers inside Rose Garden Conservatory, Indian in Ceremonial Dress, Mayfest, Woodward Park (Last Page)

Published By: Novel Idea Books

Publisher: Scott Perry

Editor-in-Chief: Howard J. Doak, II

Copywriter: J. Thomas Golden

Cover Design: David Clark

Project Management, Book Design/Layout, Book Production and Printing: Signature Graphics Corporation, Tulsa, OK

The following books were quoted or relied upon:

Butler, William.
    1974 *Tulsa 75*

Debo, Angie.
    1943 *Tulsa: From Creek Town to Oil Capital*

Inhofe-Tucker, Marilyn, Sandi Jones, and Kate Reeves.
    1995 *Footsteps Through Tulsa*

Irving, Washinton.
    1955 *A Tour on the Prairies*

Sterling,Bryan B. and Frances N. Sterling.
    1995 *Will Rogers Speaks*

Vaughn-Roberson, Courtney and Glen Vaughn-Roberson.
    1984 *City in the Osage Hills, Tulsa, Oklahoma*

Wallis, Michael.
    1990 *Route 66: The Mother Road*

Yagoda, Ben.
    1993 *Will Rogers: A Biography*

Foreword by J Thomas Golden

Tulsa… it is a name that has meant many things to many people, and its journey from trading post to cow town to a center of the American oil industry to its development into a modern cosmopolitan city is certainly as colorful and interesting as any in the world.

Long before names were placed on maps of North America, people inhabited the area that we now call Tulsa. Paleoindians of the Clovis and Folsom cultures roamed the plains of Oklahoma over 10,000 years ago hunting mammoth, bison, and other large land mammals with stone projectile points mounted on long wooden shafts. The natural bounty of the area attracted numerous Native American groups throughout prehistory, culminating with the Caddoan peoples who built large ceremonial centers with majestic earthen mounds at places like Spiro, just east of Tulsa.

In 1719 Bernard de la Harpe arrived in Oklahoma, coming within thirty miles of Tulsa and claiming the land for France. The land, a part of the Louisiana Province, was given to Spain in 1763 in return for aid during the French and Indian War. It was soon returned to France who then sold it to the young United States government on August 30, 1803 as part of the Louisiana Purchase. Seen as a wild, relatively useless land with few resources, it was quickly targeted for the relocation of Native American tribes of the East whose land was being encroached upon by white settlement. In 1817 the Cherokee began to arrive in what would soon be called Indian Territory, the beginning of a long string of migrations along the Trail of Tears which would bring the Five Civilized Tribes to Oklahoma. The area including Tulsa was given to the Creek in 1826.

In 1836 the Lochapoka Creek arrived at the end of their long march from Alabama to settle in the valley near the Arkansas River that would become Tulsa. A site was chosen on a hilltop overlooking the river and a ceremonial fire was kindled beneath a large oak tree using ashes brought from their faraway home. This is the Council Oak tree which still stands today at 17th Street and Cheyenne Avenue. The Lochapoka laid out a village, in accordance with their tradition, under the leadership of their chief, Achee Yahola. At this point the village was known as Lochapoka; however, the village soon became known as Tulsee or sometimes Tulsee Town after the third Lochapoka chief. The Lochapoka remained relatively isolated, living a simple lifestyle not much different from their life in Alabama. They hunted, fished, and grew communal fields of corn in the areas around their village, and seasonally they sent parties to take buffalo on the plains to the north. In 1848 Lewis Perryman established the first trading post in Tulsa. Perryman opened up the village to trade and increased traffic from other Creek and Osage passersby. He built a large house at 33rd Street and Rockford Avenue, and soon became a successful rancher and businessman. He and his offspring were to be prominent players in Tulsa history for many years.

The United States Civil War was a confusing and difficult time for the residents of Tulsa. With attentions focused elsewhere, the Union government all but abandoned Indian Territory, leaving Confederates the opportunity to win the Creek, Cherokee, and several other tribes, many of whom owned slaves, over to their cause. Five of the Perryman sons joined the Confederacy. Allegiance to the South was not unanimous though. Many Creek and other tribesmen remained loyal to the Union, and pleaded with officials for assistance. Eager to escape the turmoil of war, a mass migration of people was begun from Indian Territory to the safety of Union forts in Kansas. Tulsa was abandoned at this time and its people largely avoided the battles that were to take place between the opposing tribesmen and their white allies. Lewis Perryman died in Kansas, but his sons, who had deserted the Confederates and joined their father, returned to help resettle Tulsa.

Perhaps the most formidable obstacle between Tulsa and the oil boom was the Arkansas River, which other than the railroad could only be crossed by an unreliable ferry or over a river ford. When the City could not raise the funds necessary to build a bridge, three Tulsans privately financed the project and opened a toll bridge in 1904. Another group of Tulsans founded the Commercial Club with the goal of ensuring that Tulsa benefit from oil development. With a series of shrewd deals, they were able to assure that a total of four railroads and around twenty trains per day passed through Tulsa. Others sought to ensure that Tulsa was a convenient and comfortable place for oilmen to base their operations. The five-story First National Bank Building opened in 1906, followed by a new five-story Robinson Hotel, providing the necessary accommodations for the oil boom. In order to encourage field workers to live in Tulsa, a special fifteen car train, dubbed Coal Oil Johnny, was established to run laborers as far as Okmulgee and return them each day. Arguably the most notable accomplishment of the Commercial Club was their work in establishing the first refinery in 1907. The operation was small and at first a little disappointing, but served to fix Tulsa's place in the petroleum industry and eventually earn her the name of The Oil Capital of the World.

When the bell of the of the First Presbyterian Church rang in honor of Oklahoma's admission to the Union on November 16, 1907, the City of Tulsa was well positioned for the growth that would bring it to its current prominence. Development for the next two decades was extraordinary. Tulsa became the center for much of the nation's petroleum industry and many of the other industries that supported it. Profits were great, and those responsible were to immortalize themselves through both building and civic projects of grand scale. Downtown became a showplace of office building development, with no expense spared to create these monuments to prosperity. At the height of building in 1927, an average of $1 million per month was spent on downtown construction. The homes of Tulsa's business leaders were equally impressive, exhibiting all of the grandeur accorded to the new Oil Capital. Much of the public, and some private architecture, took on a new style which was as fresh as the money in Tulsa. Though many buildings featured revivals of classic styles, Tulsans became fond of the modern, geometric designs and stylized detail of art deco. Many versions of this theme were explored in buildings constructed from the late 1920's through 1930's. Today, Tulsa has one of the largest and most exemplary existing collections of art deco architecture in the world. Boston Avenue Methodist Church, the Union Depot, the old Warehouse Market, and the Spotlight Theatre are examples of the diverse art deco designs present in Tulsa.

From the beginning, Tulsa's oil men took great pride in their new community, and most became notable philanthropists. Names like Harwell, McFarlin, Skelly, Chapman, Tyrrell, Page, Kemp, and Phillips became synonymous with great wealth and generous giving. Charles Page, who had seen hard times himself, founded a home for widows and orphans at Sand Springs. Then he miraculously created an industrial city at the site to support the home. Waite Phillips, who along with his brothers attained legendary wealth in the petroleum industry, financed numerous building projects, such as downtown's Philtower, and gave land and large endowments to many organizations, including the Boy Scouts. Phillips was also to give his spacious Italian-style palace to the City for use as a museum; Philbrook Art Center and Indian Museum opened to the public in 1939.

This sense of civic duty is present in the scale of many Tulsa works. Between 1914 and 1930 most of Tulsa's religious congregations moved to spacious new homes. Notable among these are the Holy Family Cathedral, Christ the King, and Boston Avenue Methodist Church Central High School was expanded in 1922 to meet the needs of the booming population, and bonds were passed for the building of eleven additional schools to accommodate future growth. The 1920's also brought an end to the inadequacies of unreliable and sometimes contaminated water sources. In 1922 construction was begun on the Spavinaw Lake reservoir and water system which brought clean, reliable drinking water to the city. Henry Kendall College, which moved to Tulsa from Muskogee in 1907, became The University of Tulsa in 1920, and with the help

of many prominent families, obtained a permanent endowment which today stands at over $500 million. The university quite appropriately became the home of a world renowned petroleum engineering program; a reputation it maintains.

The 1920's appeared a happy carefree time for Tulsa. The national economy was high and Tulsa's was even higher. Yet, this economic success was largely inaccessible to the African American population. Segregation was in full effect, with Tulsa blacks living in a separate area of town with their own stores, schools, churches, and community endeavors. By this time the Greenwood area, which was home to the majority of this population, had become quite prosperous, enjoying such cultural riches as to be compared with New York City's Harlem district of the same time and given the nickname "The Black Wall Street." However, separate was certainly not equal. This became painfully clear after World War I, when black soldiers, performing just as bravely as whites, were segregated and enjoyed few benefits or rewards for their loyalty.

These inequalities contributed to a mounting racial tension in Tulsa which erupted violently with the Race Riots of 1921. On the evening of June 1, 1921, the *Tulsa Tribune* ran a short article covering the arrest of a black man, Dick Rowland, charged with assaulting a white female elevator attendant. When news reached the community at Greenwood that whites would storm the jailhouse and lynch Rowland, chaos ensued. Fist fights broke out when black and white mobs met at 1st and Cincinnati, followed by the groups taking up arms against one another and beginning a guerrilla war in Greenwood. Despite attempts at intervention by the National Guard, heavily armed whites took the offensive, slaughtering blacks in a hail of machine gun fire and burning much of Greenwood to the ground. Only after $2.5 million in property was destroyed, perhaps as many as 500 killed and hundreds more wounded, and after the black contingent had surrendered, was the National Guard able to take control and begin restoring order. Martial law was declared and the military took control of the city government. Ironically, Dick Rowland was released when his accuser failed to testify against him, and all charges were dropped. The rehabilitation of Greenwood would take years, and provide a chance for blacks and whites to set aside differences and work together as neighbors. Racial violence was to raise its head other times in the coming years, and gross inequality for blacks would continue, but tensions never again raged to the point of the 1921 riots thanks to both black and white leaders who took proactive roles towards ensuring that the two communities peacefully coexist.

When the stock market crashed in October of 1929, Tulsans were undaunted, most thinking that they had escaped the economic tragedy that had hit most of the nation so hard. In fact, at this time Tulsa was noted as the richest per capita and fastest growing city in the world! However, business leaders were becoming increasingly aware that they had miscalculated by developing an economy almost entirely dependent on the oil industry. When new oil fields were discovered in Seminole, Oklahoma City, and East Texas in 1930, oil reserves grew far beyond the need of a nation in the throes of the Great Depression. Oil prices dropped to as low as one cent per barrel, and Tulsa's economy, which had seemed unstoppable for so many years, crumbled.

Soon workers were being let go, businesses were closing, and Tulsans were in disbelief that their lives had changed so quickly. The pioneering spirit of Tulsa was still alive, though, and soon many efforts were underway to help those affected most by the crisis. Relief agencies joined forces to provide for those left hungry or homeless, and government officials organized to discover means to put the unemployed back to work. In 1932 the Mohawk Plan began, using city funds for a work project creating a reservoir and recreational facilities at Mohawk Park. Money was not adequate to last indefinitely and Tulsa's unemployment rate was climbing to nearly forty percent. Like most of the country, Tulsa found little help from the federal government under Herbert Hoover. Thus, on a tide of discontent, Tulsans helped to oust Hoover in the election of 1932, bringing in Franklin D. Roosevelt and the era of the New Deal.

Federal money began to roll in to continue financing the Mohawk Plan and support other building plans. Then in 1935 Roosevelt established the Works Progress Administration (WPA). This brought even more funding to Tulsa allowing for numerous projects throughout the city, and employing thousands. WPA projects improved Tulsa streets and sanitation facilities, provided direct relief to the poor, and supported the building of low cost housing and public facilities, such as Daniel Webster and Will Rogers high schools, built in 1937. The New Deal, however, was not a cure-all and economic troubles would continue to resurface.

Then, the broken spirits of the Great Depression were boosted by a frenzy of production for the national defense effort with the dawn of World War II. Tulsa became the site for the manufacture of numerous products of military concern, including aircraft, and of course, petroleum products. The great demand to fuel the engines of World War II helped bring this industry to prominence once again. Tulsa had begun contemplating expansion of its aviation industry and airfields with the first rumors that the United States would join the war, but was divided as to whether this should be done by expanding the Municipal Airport built in 1928, or by establishing a new facility. It had been decided that expansion of Municipal Airport would be the most prudent route, until news came of the Japanese bombing of Pearl Harbor on December 7, 1941. Tulsans quickly voted to fund both this expansion and the addition of a second airport. At this time, the Spartan School of Aeronautics, founded in 1928 by W. G. Skelly, gained much recognition, training pilots and mechanics for the United States Army, as well as, pilots for the British Royal Air Force.

Expansion of industry to meet war needs meant enduring additional hard times for Tulsans. Food was rationed along with fuel and other products allocated mainly for military consumption. But the economic boost and patriotic sense of community created by the war rallied Tulsans to face the challenges and prepare for the future. Plans were immediately begun for turning wartime industries into profitable peacetime endeavors and to accommodate the needs of returning veterans. Tulsa, perhaps for the first time, began to give significant attention to careful planning for future growth.

The 1950's saw Tulsa continue to grow at a steady rate with an economy that seemed resilient against national fluxes. Business, though still dominated by oil, began to see increased diversification. After the 1954 *Brown vs. Topeka Board of Education* decision, Tulsa began the process of desegregating its schools and communities. This was not accomplished without resistance, and would not be satisfactorily complete until the mid-1970's. In 1957, The University of Tulsa celebrated its 50th graduating class and announced a $5 million drive for new facilities. Tulsans expressed their commitment to educational and cultural enrichment by meeting this need, as well as improving facilities for Gilcrease Museum, created from the collections of Thomas Gilcrease, purchased by the city in 1955. Thus began a movement to make Tulsa the cultural center of Oklahoma and a leader in the Southwest. Support was given to a symphony, and ballet and theatre troupes were brought in from around the country.

The 1960's through the 1980's saw Tulsa grow phenomenally on all fronts. Construction, business development, and population growth rivaled that of the oil boom, and Tulsa business finally obtained true diversity. Thus, Tulsa did not suffer greatly when many oil companies packed up and moved operations to Houston. Tulsa was no longer the Oil Capital of the World, but it was still fiscally strong, as demonstrated by its ability to take the coming times of inflation and recession in stride. Tulsa business was also boosted by the completion of the Arkansas River Navigational System in 1971, connecting Tulsa to the world by water, land, rail, and air. This period also saw Tulsans strive to improve their public schools and limit the inequalities of race and class while augmenting civic and cultural initiatives to make Tulsa a cosmopolitan oasis of the Southwest.

Today, Tulsa bears the fruit that its founders and supporters have worked so hard for throughout the years. Tulsa is similar to many other cities its size with a distinct downtown and sprawling residential, business, and industrial sectors. Over time, it has incorporated smaller towns and now adjoins suburban areas to create a metropolitan area with over 750,000 inhabitants. Yet, Tulsa maintains a spirit that sets it apart from all others. This spirit might best be described as the overwhelming sense of individualism and community pride that harkens back to Tulsa's pioneer past. This spirit makes Tulsa a truly interesting and enriching place to live. It has an atmosphere ripe for exploring new ideas and concepts while still managing to adhere to the conservative background it has boasted since its founding.

Tulsa has also maintained the commitment to education and cultural endeavors begun so many years ago. It hosts three universities, medical school facilities, junior colleges, vocational schools, private schools, and an outstanding public school system. The lives of Tulsans are enriched by Philbrook and Gilcrease museums, and other special interest museums and galleries, such as, the notable collections of the Fenster Museum of Jewish Art. The Tulsa Philharmonic, Tulsa Metropolitan Opera, Tulsa Ballet Theatre, and dozens of other theatrical and artistic organizations create a wealth of opportunities to enjoy the arts available in few cities of Tulsa's size. Tulsa also attracts national and international entertainers of all genres. All of this is combined with a schedule of special events and festivals for Tulsans to enjoy year round. Popular among these are the annual Mayfest, Reggaefest, the Boom River Fourth of July Celebration, Greenwood Jazz Festival, and Oktoberfest.

Perhaps Tulsa's development can adequately be summed up with a story told by Angie Debo in her 1943 history of the city. Debo tells of a man visiting from California in 1941 who had not seen Tulsa in nearly 40 years. He was I. L. Harness, one of the drillers of the Red Fork strike in 1901. Mr. Harness first went to Red Fork, which by 1941 had become an industrial section. Next, he walked through downtown among skyscrapers holding the headquarters of some of the world's most important corporations, and among the hustle and bustle of a big city. Mr. Harness could only remark that Tulsa had changed since he had last seen it. Of course, if Mr. Harness or many of the dozens of others who helped pave the way for Tulsa's success could see it today, they would truly be amazed.

Yes, Tulsa has indeed changed from its humble beginnings as a Creek Indian village to its early days as a town participating in the cattle trade of the Southwest, which, with that fortuitous discovery in 1901, soon became the Oil Capital of the World and grew into the beautiful city with the special attitude that it is today. Thus, it seems that "change" should be a special word for Tulsans, for it is the lifeblood of the city and the force that guides it into the future.

Harwelden, an English Gothic Tudor built in 1923 for oil baron Earl Palmer Harwell, now serves as the home of the Arts and Humanities Council of Tulsa, and is a venue for many social events, weddings and receptions.

Realizing the potential of the little race car ride he built for his son's birthday, Robert Bell, Sr. began marketing his children's ride around the city. By 1951, the rides had become popular enough for Bell to move his rides to Tulsa County Fairgrounds and establish Bell's Amusement Park. Today, Bell's is part of a large entertainment complex between 15th and 21st Street near Yale Avenue that includes the Tulsa County Fairgrounds, Fair Meadows Race Track, Driller Stadium, and Big Splash Waterpark.

The old Warehouse Market, with its impressive Art Deco tower, stands at 11th Street and Elgin. This recently refurbished building is now home to Lyon's Indian Store and a local Italian restaurant.

S ince 1984 Novel Idea Bookstores, with locations at 71st and Sheridan and 51st and Harvard, has been Tulsa's premier Book Haven. Novel Idea is
one of the many unique stores which make Tulsa a popular shopping destination for miles around.

T he Council Oak Tree at 18th and Cheyenne, standing on the site as
early as 1836, is a gentle reminder of Tulsa's past as a part of Indian
Territory. At the end of their long march from Alabama on the Trail of
Tears, members of the Creek tribe continued the tradition of a ceremonial
fire at the foot of the tree. Tribe members brought the live coals from
Alabama to recognize their new home which eventually would become
Tulsa. (◄ Photo Left)

Weber's Root Beer stand, located at 3817 South Peoria, has been owned and operated by the Bilby family since they established it in 1933. Many young people "cruising" Brookside looked for the Weber's sign knowing it promised cold, frosty glasses of homemade root beer.

The painstakingly crafted Spanish-style terra cotta facade, with whimsical griffins and gargoyles among its motifs, makes the Martindale Tulsa's most ornate building. Shortly after its completion in 1927, the Martindale, originally a hotel, hosted guests from around the world attending Tulsa's International Petroleum Exposition.

Tulsa architect Frank W. Wallace's Prayer Tower, with its radiating spires, stands as a centerpiece of the Oral Roberts University campus. ORU, located at 81st and Lewis, officially opened in 1965.

Tulsa is blessed with great enthusiasm for the arts, hosting professional orchestra, opera and ballet companies. Ballet gained a permanent and prominent position when world renowned dancers Moscelyne Larkin and Roman Jasinski founded Tulsa Ballet Theatre in 1956. Since this time, the company has received national and international acclaim for its innovation and ties to the Ballet Russe tradition of its founders. Tulsa Ballet moved to a newly renovated facility in 1992, prompting *The New York Times* to denote the occasion as one of the 25 memorable dance events of the year, calling the move a "reason to rejoice."

S t. John's Hospital at 21st Street and Utica Avenue was established by the Sisters of the Sorrowful Mother in 1926 to meet the needs of a Tulsa that was becoming increasingly more urban. The west wing of the hospital is the only surviving portion of the original building.

T ulsa's old Federal Building with the apropos Federal-styled facade of many government and public buildings throughout the nation, complete with imposing Corinthian columns, adds a noble element to downtown Tulsa. (► Photo Right)

The home of Thomas Gilcrease, whose remarkable collections formed the beginnings of the museum, is located on the grounds of Gilcrease Museum.

The entrance to Gilcrease Museum is graced by Sacred Rain Arrow, the work of Native American sculptor Allen Houser. Houser is the great nephew of Apache chief, Geronimo.

Tulsa thrives with a spirit of volunteerism and community service. In times of crisis or need, you will always find Tulsa firemen ready to lend a helping hand.

When completed in 1918, the 16-story Cosden Building, later renamed the Mid-Continent Building, was the tallest concrete structure or "skyscraper", in the country. The "Prince of Petroleum," Josh Cosden, erected the building on the site of Tulsa's first school, the 1884 Mission. The project was completed for a total of one million dollars. An additional 30 floors were added in the 1980's. (◄ Photo Left)

Tucked into the Ozark foothills outside the city, Lake Spavinaw was built in 1922 to supply the needs of a rapidly growing Tulsa. Today the reservoir is still an important water source, as well as a space for fishing and other outdoor recreation.

The majestic 258-foot tower of the Boston Avenue Methodist Church pierces the Tulsa skyline. At its completion in 1927, it was the first church in the country to be built according to American style architecture. It is still noted as an exemplary piece of Art Deco architecture and is one of the finest examples of cathedrals in the world. The church has also been placed on the National Registry of Historic Places. (◄ Photo Left)

Washington Irving was the American Ambassador to Spain for several years, earning him the recognition of being America's most famous man of letters. In 1832 Irving joined the Ellsworth expedition on a tour of the American frontier, a journey that brought him through what is now Tulsa. The Washington Irving Monument marks the spot where he surveyed the Tulsa surroundings and said, "It seems to me as if these beautiful regions answer literally to the description of the land of promise, a land flowing with milk and honey."

Just a short drive away, Tulsa area lakes and streams provide a getaway for activities such as boating, fishing and swimming. Tulsa's lakes and rivers, in combination with the rest of the state of Oklahoma, make up 11,846 miles of shoreline, more shoreline than any other state in the entire United States of America.

The American buffalo was a mainstay of both the diet and spiritual life of many Native American tribes for thousands of years before European exploration. Herds of thousands of buffalo once roamed the plains around Tulsa. Then the introduction of the gun, horse, and the European idea of hunting for sport brought the mighty buffalo to near extinction. Extensive efforts are now being made to reintroduce these animals into their native habitat.

The Walter Arts Center, featuring a 1,200 seat main theater, dance and studio theaters, a gallery, and practice space, is the focal point of Holland Hall's arts program. The school has been offering a co-educational experience emphasizing academics, the arts, and sports since 1922. Holland Hall's education is geared towards the individual student's needs. This is one of the many reasons why the school boasts an almost 100% college attendance rate.

Frank Lloyd Wright, perhaps America's most celebrated architect, designed the 1919 Westhope for his cousin Richard Lloyd Jones. The 10,000 square foot home built for Jones, owner of *The Tulsa Tribune*, is much larger than the typical Wright house, but is designed to seem cozy for small groups of people or accommodate gatherings of up to 400. The two-story house, which is one of only three Frank Lloyd Wright designed structures in the state, is listed on the National Register of Historic Places.

The 52-story Bank of Oklahoma Tower is the work of New York City's World Trade Center designer, Minoru Yamasaki, and is Oklahoma's tallest office building. (►Photo Right)

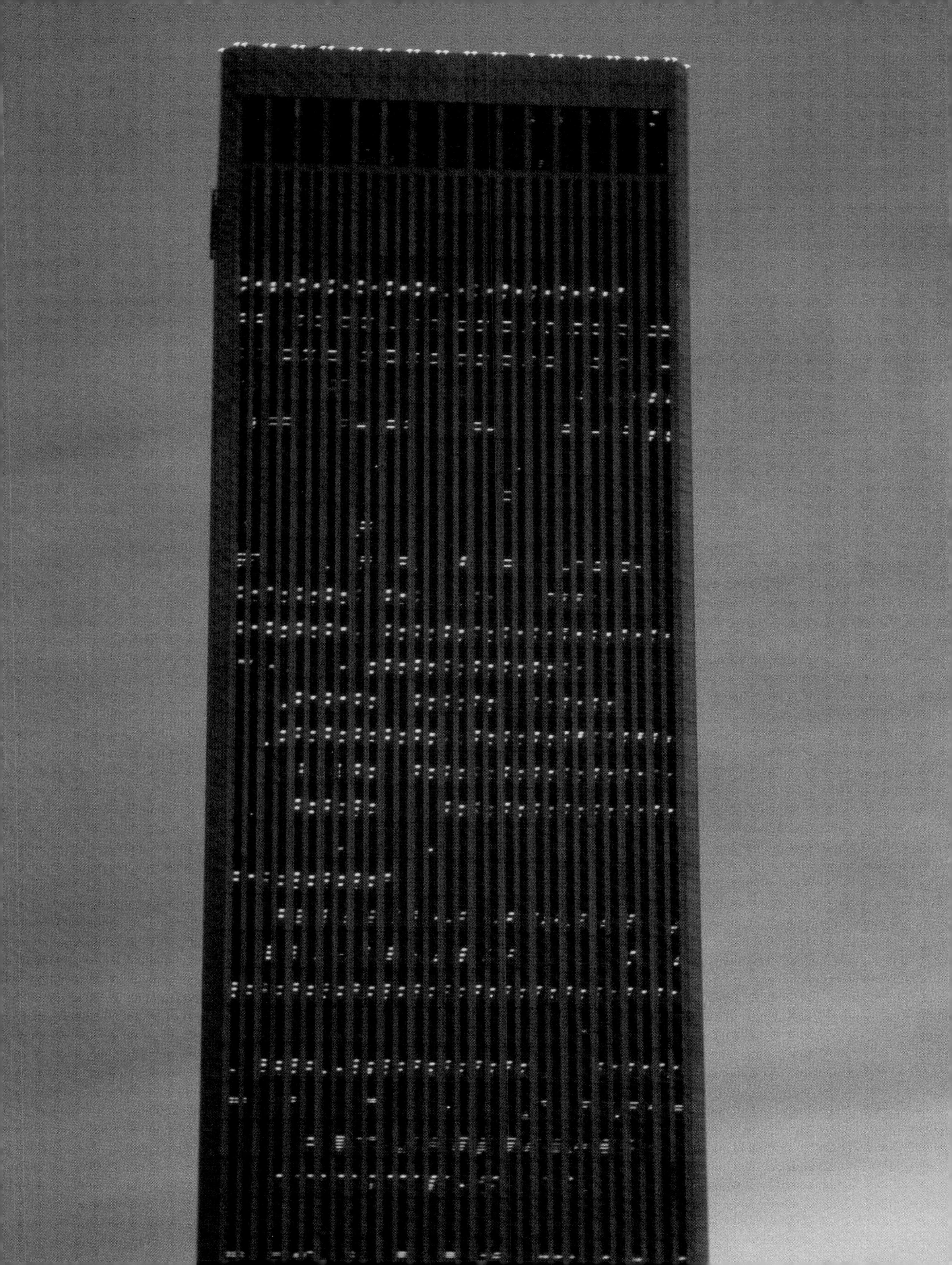

Considered one of the most beautiful cities in the United States, Tulsa is a botanists delight. Located where the eastern Woodlands meet the Great Plains, Tulsa is a place to watch many hardwood species display their bright fall shades of crimson, gold and orange.

Vernon African Methodist Episcopal Church houses Tulsa's oldest African American congregation. The church emerged out of the work of pioneers who brought African Methodism to Tulsa Indian Territory as early as 1905. The original structure at 309 North Greenwood was destroyed during the 1921 race riots; reconstruction was begun less than a year later.

Tulsa may be the "big city" to many, but it has never lost its ties to the Old West. Rodeo events, such as this one at the Tulsa State Fairgrounds, always draw large crowds.

A symbol of the bygone era of railroad travel, the Union Depot, built in 1931, has been painstakingly restored to provide office space while maintaining the architectural integrity of this Art Deco masterpiece. Tulsa boasts one of the finest collections of Art Deco architecture in the nation. (◄ Photo Left)

The Liddy Doenges Wall, with its florid display of forsythias, memorializes one of Tulsa's great supporters of the arts. Mrs. Doenges served on the board of directors of The Arts & Humanities Council of Tulsa for 18 years. Her commitment to the organization prompted it to rename its annual award, recognizing individual contributions to the arts and humanitites in her memory.

The modern office spaces at Warren Place, near 61st Street and Yale Avenue, are symbolic of the recent growth of South Tulsa.

The stately Jacobethan McBirney Mansion at 14th Street and Galveston Avenue was built in 1927 for Tulsa developer, banker, and baseball player James H. McBirney. An Irish immigrant and former janitor, McBirney and his brother Sam opened the Bank of Commerce in 1905; the name was later changed to National Bank of Commerce.

The Brook Theatre neon sign has been an icon of entertainment in the popular Brookside area since the 1940's. The theatre hosted long engagements of numerous Rodgers & Hammerstein musicals, as well as the world premiere of "The Sound of Music," before becoming a restaurant and bar.

Stretching a combined nine miles on either side of the Arkansas River, River Parks attracts over 800,000 visitors each year. River Parks provides outdoor enthusiasts with a myriad of recreational activities including jogging and biking trails, picnic areas, playgrounds, and venues for major events and festivals.

Tulsa, a thriving metropolitan area with a population of over 750,000, is surrounded by sprawling countryside including prairies, forests, lakes, streams, and rolling hills. (◄ Photo Left)

M any of Tulsa's downtown buildings were built during the economic high of the oil boom, with no expense spared and great attention given to the smallest detail. The highly ornamented buildings display elaborate moldings, friezes, bas-relief, and other accoutrements, like this clock on the Mid-Continent Building.

The Greenwood Cultural Center in the historic Greenwood District North of downtown houses the Oklahoma Jazz Hall of Fame. The Greenwood District is famous and infamous for being counted among the birthplaces of jazz, and a primary site of the Tulsa race riots in 1921. Today, the neighborhood is the target of renewed development and sense of pride, highlighted by the annual Greenwood Jazz Festival.

When the city purchased Woodward Park in 1909, it was widely criticized as being too far out of town. Now this tranquil oasis in the center of the city is a favorite of many Tulsans. The park's forty acres include a rock garden with over 15,000 azaleas, a formal rose garden, and a Victorian conservatory.
(►Photo Next Page)

I n 1926 Tulsans flocked to try the new five-cent sandwich known as the "Coney Island," and Greek immigrant Christ Economou's fledgling business was a success. Coney Island's new downtown location at 4th Street and Boulder Avenue still provides a fast, economical lunch for business people.

The unique Tulsa skyline combines the modern structures of today with the historical Art Deco buildings from yesterday.

The Philbrook neighborhood is graced by many stately homes and gardens, making it one of Tulsa's loveliest areas. Philbrook Museum, a Tulsa treasure, was the home of oil man Waite Phillips.

The twelve-story 320 Boston Building opened its doors in 1917. In 1923 a twelve-story addition was completed, and in 1927 a tower was added, making the 320 Boston Building the tallest in Tulsa. The design of the building's tower anticipated dirigibles docking on the roof, but the trend never developed.

The French Gothic Holy Family Cathedral was dedicated in 1914, replacing an earlier Roman Catholic church built in 1899, the first permanent church building in Tulsa. The three heavenward spires of the current structure represent the cathedral's namesake.

The richly appointed Skelly Mansion at 21st Street and Madison Boulevard was bought by Tulsa oil millionaire and philanthropist William G. Skelly during its construction in 1921. The 25-room neoclassical home is the work of architect John T. Blair, designer of several of Tulsa's historic homes.

The pink facade of St. Francis Hospital at 61st Street and Yale Avenue is a familiar site to most who have spent time in Tulsa. St. Francis' commitment to quality care and state-of-the-art technology have earned it the reputation as one of the top 100 hospitals in the country.

Yahola Lake, located in Mohawk Park, invokes the spirit of Tulsa's earliest settlers. The traditions of the Lochapoka Creek Indian, who, in 1836, settled in what would become Tulsa, tell of a great leader named Achee Yahola, who led them from their home in Alabama and established their place in Indian Territory. Named for a Creek deity, Achee Yahola built his first cabin at the modern intersection of 1st Street and Frisco Avenue. (► Photo Next Page.)

The Atlas Life Building was designed by the architectural team of Rush, Endacott and Rush, whose work can be seen in several downtown buildings. The inverted "T" shaped building was completed in 1922, and the roof is adorned by a sculpture of the mythical Atlas holding the world.

The 40-acre wooded and beautifully landscaped grounds of Cascia Hall Preparatory School are located near 21st Street and Utica Avenue. The private Catholic co-educational day school for grades 6-12 was founded by the Order of St. Augustine in 1926. The dominant neo-French Norman architecture of the school, named for St. Rita of Cascia, includes the original 1926 monastery and classroom building.

After the cold, wet months of winter, springtime in Tulsa affords many the chance to take to their gardens.

A number of the world's most important companies have called Tulsa home throughout the years, and their legacy has been much more than the economic verve that has made the city prosper. Tulsa businesses, big and small, take a keen interest in the community through charitable contributions and endeavors to beautify their urban setting.

In 1913 the citizens of Tulsa passed a $100,000 bond issue to build the city's first convention hall. Brady Theatre was completed the following year.
Elvis Presley, Will Rogers, Katherine Hepburn, Ed Sullivan, Anna Pavlova, Bette Midler, and Maya Angelou are just a few of the celebrities who have entertained audiences at the hall, affectionately known as "the Old Lady on Brady."

Beginning as a rapid, snow-fed mountain stream, easily crossed by foot, near Leadville, Colorado, the Arkansas River has played numerous roles in Tulsa's history. It was considered a great beauty and important resource to the city's early Native American settlers and a nuisance that couldn't be predictably crossed until a private wagon bridge was built in 1904 by white pioneers. Indeed, the heavily polluted, shallow course was ridiculed for many years, prompting Will Rogers to remark that, "Paving the Arkansas would be cheaper than making it navigable." Great effort has been made in recent years to clean up the river and make it a beautiful backdrop for the city.

Located just northwest of downtown, the area that is now Owen Park provided a tranquil setting as early as 1825 when it was the site for the signing of a treaty for the relocation of the Five Civilized Tribes. Today, Owen Park offers space for outdoor activities and events centered around the North American Continent Building and a lake stocked with fish.

Nelson's Buffeteria has been the place to dine for the business person on the go since Nelson Rodgers, Sr. opened the original location at 4th Street and Main in 1929. Nelson Rodgers, II maintains the business at 514 South Boston.

In 1904 Tulsa's golf course was located on a lease near where Hillcrest Medical Center stands today. The landlord was an old Indian woman remembered for shooing wandering golfers from her backyard with her Winchester rifle. In 1908 the course moved to its present location in Osage Hills and became known as Tulsa Country Club. The club grew, along with Tulsa, redesigning and updating its golf course and adding facilities for numerous social and recreational activities through the years. (► Photo Next Page)

This archway in historic Osage Hills, located at Fairview and Osage, makes a perfect frame for Tulsa's beautiful skyline.

Though the Greenwood District's place in Tulsa history is marred by the disastrous occurrences of the 1921 Race Riot, the area today is a point of pride for the city. Ambitious revitalization programs and the diligent work of residents of the neighborhood have served to create a community rich in culture and heritage. From its establishment Greenwood has played a big role in the development of jazz, blues and Dixieland music. The role of music in Greenwood's history is celebrated annually with the Juneteenth Celebration and the Greenwood Jazz Festival, both of which draw big name performers and large audiences.

Oklahoma's favorite son, Will Rogers, was born near Oolagah, just outside Tulsa, in 1879. Rogers was perhaps the world's first superstar, getting his start in a vaudeville cowboy act before moving on to the famous Ziegfeld Folllies. He was killed in an airplane crash near Point Barrow, Alaska in 1935. By this time the 55 year old Rogers had become an international figure with a radio show, a daily syndicated newspaper column, and starring roles in several motion pictures. His untimely death was mourned nationwide with as much reverence as is given to U.S. Presidents.

The Lord and Burnham style Woodward Park Conservatory stands behind the Tulsa Garden Center, located in a home which has been occupied by several prominent families. One of the mistresses of the house used the conservatory, completed in 1926, exclusively for growing orchids. The structure is now maintained as part of Woodward Park and contains seasonal flower displays and permanent displays of tropical plants and collections of cacti and succulents from arid regions of the world.

As a city, Tulsa has alternately dismissed and embraced its ties to its Native American heritage. Today, located near the homes of numerous tribes, Tulsa has come to celebrate Native America with renewed pride. People of all backgrounds enjoy the many annual pow wows and festivals designed to preserve the languages and customs of America's oldest cultures. Tulsa and its surrounding areas are also a popular tourist destination for those coming to witness Native American crafts, monuments, and events, and for natives from other states coming to visit and commune with other tribespeople.

Mayfest is one of the most popular of Tulsa's many annual celebrations. Thousands from Tulsa and the surrounding area flock to downtown for the ten-day event to enjoy the outdoor art exhibits, crafts, food, and free concerts from local and nationally renowned performers.

The rock gardens at Woodward Park were built in 1930 using native honeycombed limestone from just outside the city. The stream that flows through the garden is constructed from concrete and overlaid with stones to give the natural appearance of a springfed brook trickling to the foot of a wooded hill where it flows into a bog garden. The lower portions of the gardens are allowed to retain a wild character, while the upper garden is carefully maintained with seasonal flower plantings, bronze mythological sculpture and a dolphin fountain.
(► Photo Next Page)